BROOKS ROBINSON
THIRD BASEMAN

BALTIMORE
ORIOLES

EARL WEAVER
MANAGER

BALTIMORE
ORIOLES

THE STORY OF THE BALTIMORE ORIOLES

Published by Creative Education
P.O. Box 227, Mankato, Minnesota 56002
Creative Education is an imprint of The Creative Company
www.thecreativecompany.us

Design and production by Blue Design
Art direction by Rita Marshall
Printed by Corporate Graphics in the United States of America

Photographs by Corbis (Bettmann), Getty Images (Lisa Blumenfeld, Linda Cataffo/NY Daily News Archive, Diamond Images, Jerry Driendl, Focus on Sport, Bob Gomel/Time & Life Pictures, John Grieshop/MLB Photos, Harry How, Brad Mangin/MLB Photos, Hunter Martin, Ted Mathias/AFP, J. Meric, Ronald C. Modra/Sports Imagery, Hy Peskin/Time & Life Pictures, Photofile/MLB Photos, Rich Pilling/MLB Photos, Jamie Squire, Perry Thorsvik, Tony Tomsic/MLB Photos, Peter Stackpole/Time & Life Pictures, Tim Umphrey, Dilip Vishwanat, Hank Walker/Time & Life Pictures)

Library of Congress Cataloging-in-Publication Data

Gilbert, Sara.
The story of the Baltimore Orioles / by Sara Gilbert.
p. cm. — (Baseball: the great American game)
Includes index.
Summary: The history of the Baltimore Orioles professional baseball team from its inaugural 1902 season as the St. Louis Browns to today, spotlighting the team's greatest players and most memorable moments.
ISBN 978-1-60818-033-2
1. Baltimore Orioles (Baseball team)—History—Juvenile literature. 2. St. Louis Browns (Baseball team)—History—Juvenile literature. I. Title. II. Series.

GV875.B2G55 2011
796.357'640975271—dc22   2010023562

CPSIA: 110310 PO1381

First Edition
9 8 7 6 5 4 3 2 1

Page 3: Right fielder Frank Robinson
Page 4: Pitcher Jeremy Guthrie

BASEBALL: THE GREAT AMERICAN GAME

THE STORY OF THE BALTIMORE ORIOLES

Sara Gilbert

CREATIVE EDUCATION

CONTENTS

CHAPTERS

Baseball in Baltimore 6

A Pair of Robinsons 15

Taking Flight 21

A New Nest 26

Earning Their Wings 36

AROUND THE HORN

Little Eddie at the Bat 12

The Trade 20

Birds on the Hill 24

An All-Star Welcome 31

The Home Run That Wasn't 38

A Family Affair 45

ALL-TIME ORIOLES

P — Jim Palmer 8

C — Chris Hoiles 13

1B — Eddie Murray 14

2B — Davey Johnson 18

3B — Brooks Robinson 27

SS — Cal Ripken Jr. 28

LF — John Lowenstein 30

CF — Brady Anderson 35

RF — Paul Blair 39

M — Earl Weaver 40

Index 48

BASEBALL IN BALTIMORE

The city of Baltimore, Maryland, has played an important role in the history of the United States. It was the site of the Second Continental Congress, where George Washington was christened as the country's leader, in 1775. The first U.S. naval ship was launched from its port in 1797, Francis Scott Key wrote the words to "The Star Spangled Banner" there in 1814, and the first Roman Catholic cathedral in the country was built there in 1821. Baltimore was the birthplace of renowned author Edgar Allan Poe, longtime Supreme Court justice Thurgood Marshall, and U.S. congresswoman Nancy Pelosi.

Baltimore is also important to the history of baseball as the birthplace of Babe Ruth, one of the most celebrated players of all time. The slugger had had several opportunities to play against the St. Louis Browns, the team that arrived in his hometown in 1954 under the new Orioles name, by the time his career with the Boston Red Sox and the New York Yankees was complete. He is even reported to have applied to manage the Browns, who joined the American League (AL) in 1902, in 1938.

A notable seaport, the city of Baltimore has a rich history of shipbuilding and remains a major destination in commercial shipping today.

PITCHER · JIM PALMER

Known for his high-kick delivery, Jim Palmer played his entire big-league career in an Orioles uniform and holds club records for strikeouts, wins, shutouts, and complete games. Over his 19-year career, he also assembled a remarkable 2.86 earned run average (ERA). In 1966, his first season as a regular in the Orioles' rotation, he became the youngest pitcher ever (just under 21 years of age) to hurl a complete-game shutout in the World Series. After missing the 1968 season with an injury, he went on to become a 20-game winner in 8 seasons and to capture the Cy Young Award 3 times (1973, 1975, and 1976).

STATS

Orioles seasons: 1965–67, 1969–84

Height: 6-foot-3

Weight: 190

- **268–152 career record**
- **2,212 career strikeouts**
- **6-time All-Star**
- **Baseball Hall of Fame inductee (1990)**

JIM PALMER
PITCHER

BALTIMORE
ORIOLES

Although the Browns finished dead last in the league 14 times during their 52 years in St. Louis, Missouri, they enjoyed a sensational season in 1922. But it wasn't just their 93–61 record that was impressive; with 39 home runs, left fielder Ken Williams bested Ruth's total of 35 for the home run crown. But Ruth and his Yankees won the bigger prize, taking the AL pennant over the Browns by a single game.

St. Louis finally broke into the postseason in 1944, when All-Star shortstop Vern Stephens helped lead the 89–65 Browns to the pennant. In the World Series, the Browns faced their crosstown rivals, the St. Louis Cardinals, in what became known as the "Trolley Series" or "Streetcar Series." The Browns were underdogs, but the bulk of the fans were on their side. "It kind of surprised me, because we drew more fans than the Browns during the season," Cardinals legend Stan Musial said afterwards. Despite widespread support, the Browns fell to the Cardinals four games to two, losing their first and only chance at a World Series title.

The team returned to its losing ways for the rest of the decade. Then baseball magnate Bill Veeck took ownership of the Browns in 1951 and decided that it would be in their best interests to push the Cardinals

1945 BROWNS

out of town. Veeck even decorated Sportsman's Park, which the two teams shared, entirely in Browns paraphernalia. But when the locally owned Anheuser-Busch beer company purchased the Cardinals, it became clear that the Browns would be the odd team out.

That turn of events led to Veeck's decision in 1954 to sell the franchise to a group of Baltimore businessmen, who quickly relocated the club and renamed it the Baltimore Orioles, after Maryland's state bird. Dressed in black and orange in honor of their namesake's plumage, the Orioles took the field at Memorial Stadium for the first time on April 13, 1954. Yet despite the efforts of Stephens and a new trio of players netted in a trade with the Yankees—power-hitting catcher Gus Triandos, slick-fielding outfielder Gene Woodling, and shortstop Willie Miranda—the Orioles posted a 54–100 record in their first season in Baltimore. Still, fans filled the stadium game after game, providing a foundation on which the franchise could be built.

GENE WOODLING

Gene Woodling joined the Orioles in 1954 via a humongous trade with the Yankees in which a total of 17 players were swapped between the East Coast teams. In 1959, he batted .300 and represented Baltimore in the All-Star Game.

LITTLE EDDIE AT THE BAT

St. Louis Browns owner Bill Veeck was notorious for the publicity stunts he used to put fans in the seats. He once promoted "Grandstand Manager's Day," during which fans in attendance were given "Yes/No" cards and allowed to make all team decisions regarding such moves as stealing bases, bunting, and changing pitchers (the Browns won the game 5–3). But perhaps Veeck's most outrageous stunt came during the second game of a 1951 doubleheader against the Detroit Tigers. In the bottom of the first inning, Browns manager Zack Taylor sent newly signed Eddie Gaedel up to the plate as a pinch hitter. What made the substitution notable was that Gaedel was a dwarf who stood only 3-foot-7! Once the diminutive hitter's contract had been presented, the umpire allowed Gaedel, who wore jersey number 1/8, to bat. Tigers pitcher Bob Cain was laughing as he prepared to pitch to the tiniest strike zone in major-league history. Not surprisingly, Gaedel walked on four pitches and was then promptly taken out of the game for a pinch runner. Although AL president Will Harridge would void Gaedel's contract the next day, the St. Louis crowd loved the stunt, giving the small batsman a standing ovation as he left the field.

CATCHER · CHRIS HOILES

Catchers love to be known as selfless players who aren't afraid to do the dirty work to help their team win. Chris Hoiles had such a reputation. Hoiles was never an All-Star, nor did he ever win a Gold Glove award for his defense. What he brought to the team was a bit of power at the plate and a knack for getting on base. Hoiles's best season was 1993, when he hit .310 while blasting 29 home runs and driving in 82 runs. Over the course of a 10-year career with the Orioles, the fan favorite was also solid, if not spectacular, behind the plate.

CHRIS HOILES
CATCHER

BALTIMORE
ORIOLES

STATS

Orioles seasons: 1989–98

Height: 6 feet

Weight: 195

- **.262 career BA**
- **.994 career fielding percentage**
- **151 career HR**
- **122 career doubles**

FIRST BASEMAN · EDDIE MURRAY

Eddie Murray spread his wings early as an Orioles star, hitting .283 with 27 home runs and 88 RBI in his first big-league season to earn AL Rookie of the Year honors. He is commonly considered to be among the greatest switch hitters in major-league history, in the company of Yankees legend Mickey Mantle and Chipper Jones of the Atlanta Braves, due to his career totals of 3,255 hits and 504 home runs. Known for his consistency, he produced at least 75 RBI for a major-league-record 20 straight seasons. Although Murray was traded away in 1988, he returned to Baltimore in 1996 and helped the Orioles to their first playoff appearance since 1983.

EDDIE MURRAY
FIRST BASEMAN

BALTIMORE
ORIOLES

STATS

Orioles seasons: 1977–88, 1996

Height: 6-foot-2

Weight: 200

- **8-time All-Star**

- **3-time Gold Glove winner**

- **19 career grand slams**

- **Baseball Hall of Fame inductee (2003)**

A PAIR OF ROBINSONS

ith the money made from its robust fan attendance, the team began to invest heavily in its minor-league farm system. Baltimore's plan was to develop young players at the minor-league level by instilling a philosophy of solid fundamentals and professional attitude. Such a system, management believed, would ensure that the men would be prepared for the major leagues when the Orioles needed to bring up fresh players. The plan came to be known as the "Oriole Way," a principle followed to this day. "There are no shortcuts to where we want to go," said Baltimore manager Paul Richards. "We plan to build this team from the ground up."

The first great player produced by the Oriole Way was a gangly third baseman named Brooks Robinson. He made his major-league debut as an 18-year-old in 1955, but his weak bat kept him shuffling between the Orioles and the minors for 5 years. Finally, Baltimore pitchers begged management to keep Robinson with the big-league club because of his remarkable defense. In 1960, Robinson stayed, and both he and the team had a breakthrough year. Led by rookie pitcher Chuck Estrada's league-leading 18 victories, shortstop Ron Hansen's 22 homers, and Robinson's .294 batting average and Gold Glove-winning play at third base, the Orioles posted their first winning record at 89–65.

With knuckleballer Hoyt Wilhelm tossing pitches so erratic in their movement that catchers needed a specially designed mitt to handle his throws, the Orioles remained a contender through the mid-1960s, winning 90 or more games 4 times, but they could not capture the league title. Searching for the missing ingredient that would put the team over the top, Baltimore traded pitcher Milt Pappas and two other players to the Cincinnati Reds for outfielder Frank Robinson in 1965. The 30-year-old Robinson had won the 1961 National League (NL) Most Valuable Player (MVP) award, but Reds management decided that he was past his prime and traded him. It was a move Cincinnati would regret and a trade that would become known as one of the best in Orioles franchise history.

In 1966, Frank Robinson topped the AL with a .316 average, 49 home runs, and 122 runs batted in (RBI), capturing the Triple Crown (leading

Brooks Robinson was nicknamed "The Human Vacuum Cleaner" for his unparalleled ability to catch or scoop virtually any ball hit near third base. He committed only 263 career fielding errors, or about 1 per every 35 chances.

SECOND BASEMAN · DAVEY JOHNSON

Always a sure-gloved infielder, Davey Johnson developed considerable power at the plate later in his career. He played eight seasons with the Orioles, providing formidable batting and solid defense at a time when good hitting was considered merely a bonus in second basemen. He teamed with shortstop Mark Belanger to win matching Gold Gloves twice (in 1969 and 1971). After his playing days, Johnson made a name for himself as a manager for several teams. As the Orioles' skipper (in 1996 and 1997), he guided the club to two winning seasons, including trips to the playoffs both times.

DAVEY JOHNSON
SECOND BASEMAN

BALTIMORE
ORIOLES

STATS

Orioles seasons: 1965–72 (as player), 1996–97 (as manager)

Height: 6-foot-1

Weight: 170

• 4-time All-Star

• 3-time Gold Glove winner

• .981 career fielding percentage

• 3,862 career putouts

the league in all three categories). Meanwhile, Brooks Robinson added 23 home runs and 100 RBI, and young hurlers Jim Palmer and Dave McNally anchored a talented pitching staff. Behind these efforts, the Orioles soared to a pennant-clinching 97–63 record.

In the World Series, Baltimore faced the heavily favored Los Angeles Dodgers and two of the most feared pitchers in the game: Don Drysdale and Sandy Koufax. In Game 1, both Robinsons slugged home runs in a 5–2 Orioles victory. The Dodgers never recovered, and Baltimore rolled to a four-game sweep and the first world championship in franchise history. "To do that to a ballclub as good as the Dodgers is almost unthinkable," exclaimed Brooks Robinson. "I'm just glad I was here to see it."

Brooks and his teammates would not witness anything quite like that upset victory for several years. Baltimore was unable to maintain its championship ways, declining in the two years that followed its 1966 World Series win. Midway through the 1968 season, Hank Bauer was fired after just four years as manager and replaced by Earl Weaver.

THE TRADE

Throughout professional sports history, the trading of players between teams has been a constant gamble, with some trades leaving obvious winners and losers. On nearly any list of the most lopsided trades in sports history, one will find the Orioles mentioned as the clear winner in a 1965 trade with the Cincinnati Reds. Believing that Frank Robinson's best years were behind him, Reds general manager Bill DeWitt traded the 30-year-old outfielder to the Orioles for pitchers Milt Pappas and Jack Baldschun and outfielder Dick Simpson. It didn't take long for DeWitt to discover his folly. The next season, Robinson won the AL MVP award and the Triple Crown by hitting .316 with 49 home runs and 122 RBI. He went on to play another five seasons with the Orioles, helping the team reach the World Series four times. Meanwhile, Pappas posted a career 30–29 record in a Reds uniform, while Baldschun won just one game for Cincinnati. Simpson, the third piece of the deal, played only two seasons in a Reds uniform while batting under .260. The deal gave the Orioles some of the best years of a Hall of Fame career, while the Reds received only two seasons of mediocrity.

TAKING FLIGHT

Baltimore's feisty new skipper quickly set about lighting a fire under the Orioles. Although Weaver's heated conversations with both the media and umpires occasionally caused controversy, Weaver kept his teams in contention year after year and became known as "The Earl of Baltimore."

In 1969, the Orioles were back with a vengeance, storming through the regular season with a club-record 109 victories. The team's offensive power was again provided largely by the Robinsons but was also helped considerably by the booming bat of first baseman Boog Powell and the base-path speed of right fielder Paul Blair. Shortstop Mark Belanger and second baseman Davey Johnson provided Gold Glove-winning defense up the middle, and the team's pitching staff also had a fine season, with Mike Cuellar winning 23 games and Palmer chipping in 16.

After cruising to the AL Eastern Division title (the league had been split into two divisions that year), Baltimore swept the Minnesota Twins in three games in the AL Championship Series (ALCS) and advanced to face the New York Mets in the World Series. Featuring stars at nearly every position, the Orioles were heavily favored to beat the "no-name" Mets, who had just barely captured their division title. But the "Miracle Mets" proved they were no joke, upsetting Baltimore four games to one to win the World Series.

Stung by the loss, the Orioles came out swinging in 1970. Baltimore went 108–54 to capture the AL East and then defeated Minnesota again in the ALCS to reach the World Series. There the Orioles faced the mighty Cincinnati Reds, who were powered by such legendary stars as Pete Rose, Tony Perez, and Johnny Bench. The Orioles managed to win the first two games at Cincinnati by one run each and then headed back to Baltimore. Brooks Robinson put on a jaw-dropping defensive show and finished the World Series batting .429 with two home runs and six RBI to help the Orioles top the Reds in five games. "Baseball is a team game," said a stunned Weaver, "but what Brooks did is as close as I've ever seen one player come to winning a series by himself."

In 1971, the Orioles' starting pitchers put together a season for the history books. McNally (21), Palmer (20), Cuellar (20), and Pat Dobson

Fan favorite Boog Powell hit 35 home runs with 114 RBI in 1970 to power Baltimore toward a world title and to earn himself the AL MVP award.

BOOG POWELL

BIRDS ON THE HILL

The Orioles can lay claim to what might be the most dominant back-to-back pitching seasons in major-league history. In 1970, the staff was led by former Cy Young Award winner Mike Cuellar, who earned 24 wins with his devastating "palmball" pitch. Lefty Dave McNally also won 24 games, and the youngest hurler of the bunch, flamethrower Jim Palmer, added 20, along with a team-high 199 strikeouts. Together, the threesome accounted for 68 of the Orioles' 108 victories during the 1970 season. Baltimore's birds, however, were just getting warmed up. The next year, they had not 3, but 4 starters eclipse the prestigious 20-win mark. Cuellar again had

a spectacular season, winning 20 games. Palmer also won 20 contests while tallying 184 strikeouts. McNally topped each of them with 21 victories and only 5 losses. But what made 1971 even better than 1970 was Pat Dobson. A curveball specialist acquired from the San Diego Padres, Dobson also hurled his way to 20 victories. This phenomenal pitching propelled the Orioles to the 1971 World Series. The Orioles lost the series in seven games to the Pittsburgh Pirates, but their pitching could hardly be faulted; the Pirates didn't score more than five runs in any game.

(20) became the first pitching staff since the 1920 Chicago White Sox to feature four 20-game winners. That amazing starting rotation propelled the Orioles to a third consecutive World Series, this time opposite the Pittsburgh Pirates. Baltimore pushed the series to seven games behind solid pitching performances by Palmer and McNally, but there would be no championship repeat. The Pirates and their star outfielder, Roberto Clemente, won the deciding Game 7 by a 2–1 score to claim the title.

The Orioles captured division titles in 1973 and 1974 before falling in the playoffs. But by 1978, the team had changed dramatically. Powell and McNally left Baltimore in 1974, Frank Robinson retired in 1976, and Cuellar and Brooks Robinson were gone when the 1977 season ended. The old regime had bid farewell.

By 1979, a new generation of Orioles stars had stepped to the forefront. Eddie Murray was already among the best first basemen in the game, a slugger who was also solid in the field. Speedy center fielder Al Bumbry was a base-stealing marvel, and third baseman Doug DeCinces and outfielders John Lowenstein and Ken Singleton provided abundant power at the plate. The team's pitching staff was also loaded with talented youngsters such as Mike Flanagan and Dennis Martinez.

These new Orioles captured the AL East in 1979 with a 102–57 record.

After defeating the California Angels three games to one in the ALCS, Baltimore faced the Pirates in the World Series once again. The Orioles won three of the series' first five games, but behind phenomenal first baseman Willie Stargell, Pittsburgh won the last two games and the world title.

A NEW NEST

In 1982, Orioles fans witnessed a passing of the torch from one Baltimore icon to another. Earl Weaver was in his final year as manager when the team called up Cal Ripken Jr., a promising young shortstop. Ripken, whose father had been a longtime coach for Baltimore, exploded onto the major-league scene, hitting 28 homers and driving in 93 runs to capture AL Rookie of the Year honors. The hardworking Ripken also proved durable, not missing a single game after May 29 that year, beginning a streak of consecutive games played that would become his calling card.

In 1983, new manager Joe Altobelli guided the Orioles to a superb season. The team rolled to the AL East title with a 98–64 record, then defeated the Chicago White Sox three games to one to win the pennant.

THIRD BASEMAN · BROOKS ROBINSON

Brooks Robinson is widely regarded as the best third baseman in major-league history. He also ranks second (behind Cal Ripken Jr.) in the Baltimore record books for career hits, doubles, and RBI. Robinson helped lead the Orioles to 4 World Series and was an All-Star for 15 consecutive years. After spending his career with the team, his uniform number (5) was the first ever to be retired by Baltimore at the end of the 1977 season. Explaining the uncanny quickness of the defensive dynamo, Cincinnati Reds manager Sparky Anderson once said, "If I dropped this paper plate, he'd pick it up on one hop and throw me out at first."

BROOKS ROBINSON
THIRD BASEMAN

BALTIMORE
ORIOLES

STATS

Orioles seasons: 1955–77

Height: 6-foot-1

Weight: 180

- **1964 AL MVP**

- **16-time Gold Glove winner**

- **2,848 career hits**

- **Baseball Hall of Fame inductee (1983)**

SHORTSTOP · CAL RIPKEN JR.

The ultimate "Iron Man," Cal Ripken played in a record 2,632 consecutive games in the major leagues, and every one was in a Baltimore Orioles uniform. Originally a third baseman, Ripken split time between third and shortstop in Baltimore. He wasted no time in making a name for himself, hitting a home run in his very first at bat in 1981, winning AL Rookie of the Year honors following his first full season in 1982, and capturing the AL MVP award the next season. During Ripken's 21 years with Baltimore, the towering but soft-spoken shortstop was the heart of the team, leading by his hardworking example rather than by his words.

CAL RIPKEN JR.
SHORTSTOP

BALTIMORE
ORIOLES

STATS

Orioles seasons: 1981–2001

Height: 6-foot-4

Weight: 215

- 2-time AL MVP

- 19-time All-Star

- 2-time Gold Glove winner

- Baseball Hall of Fame inductee (2007)

In the World Series, Baltimore lost the opening game to the Philadelphia Phillies. But then the Orioles' veteran pitchers took control, surrendering only nine runs for the series as Baltimore won the next four games. Although Murray and catcher Rick Dempsey played well, there was no doubt that it was the men on the mound who won the 1983 World Series for the Orioles. "We have always relied on our pitchers," noted Dempsey. "When you can roll out guys like Palmer, Flanagan, and [Scott] McGregor every day, you're going to win a lot of games."

The Orioles experienced a gradual decline during the rest of the 1980s. Even as Murray and Ripken continued to excel, the team's stellar pitching staff began to fall apart. By 1988, Palmer, Flanagan, McGregor, and Dennis Martinez were gone. Without them, the Orioles suffered a major-league-record 21 straight losses at the start of the 1988 season. As the team limped through the end of the decade, plans for a new ballpark and the return of Frank Robinson as manager kept fans' spirits from plunging.

The Orioles' sluggishness continued into the early 1990s. Despite strong performances from Ripken and such newcomers as outfielder Brady Anderson and dominating right-handed pitcher Mike Mussina, Baltimore

LEFT FIELDER · JOHN LOWENSTEIN

On every great team, there are the big stars, and then there are those players who simply help the team win. John Lowenstein was one of the latter, a player who, when the game was on the line, was at his best. In 1979, he provided a pinch home run in Game 1 of the ALCS and a pinch two-run double in Game 4 of the World Series. He furthered his reputation as a clutch hitter in 1983 when he slammed a home run in Game 2 of the World Series to keep the Orioles alive and help them advance to win it all.

STATS

Orioles seasons: 1979–85

Height: 6 feet

Weight: 175

• 128 career stolen bases

• 441 career RBI

• .980 career fielding percentage

• .385 BA in 1983 World Series

JOHN LOWENSTEIN
LEFT FIELDER

BALTIMORE
ORIOLES

AN ALL-STAR WELCOME

Upon its official opening at the beginning of the 1992 season, Oriole Park at Camden Yards—a venue built with brick walls—was considered one of the most beautiful and fan-friendly ballparks in all of baseball. As a tip of the hat to the new ballpark, Major League Baseball elected to make Camden Yards home to the 1993 All-Star Game, an event that provided two of the most memorable moments in All-Star history. During the Home Run Derby, some of the game's top sluggers competed to see who could "go yard" most often. Although Texas Rangers outfielder Juan Gonzalez won the competition,

it was Seattle Mariners outfielder Ken Griffey Jr. who stole the show by becoming the first player ever to hit the B&O Warehouse building that stands 439 feet away from home plate. The next night, during the All-Star Game, Philadelphia Phillies first baseman John Kruk provided one of the most comical at bats in the history of the "Midsummer Classic." After intimidating Mariners pitcher Randy Johnson whistled a blazing fastball behind Kruk's head, the husky Kruk moved to the outside of the batter's box and flailed wildly for the rest of the at bat in exaggerated fear of Johnson's heater.

RAFAEL PALMEIRO

Rafael Palmeiro (above) and Mike Mussina (opposite) were Baltimore teammates for five seasons, giving the Orioles excellent infield defense.

MIKE MUSSINA

only hovered close to a winning record each year. In 1992, the team moved from Memorial Stadium into its new, baseball-only facility, Oriole Park at Camden Yards. Camden Yards was a simple yet stunning throwback to the earlier days of baseball that was embraced by fans and soon mimicked by other franchises around the league. Perhaps inspired by the new facility, the Orioles responded with two straight winning seasons.

In 1994, the Orioles added slugging first baseman Rafael Palmeiro to the roster and were in pursuit of a division title until a players' strike in August ended the season early. The following year, the team took a step backward with a third-place finish in the AL East, though fans were treated to a special night on September 6 as Ripken surpassed Lou "The

Iron Horse" Gehrig's consecutive-game mark by playing in his 2,131st straight game. Ripken's record would continue until September 20, 1998. His streak of 2,632 consecutive games played stands as one of baseball's most impressive records—one that may never be broken.

Driven by the great play of Ripken, Palmeiro, Anderson, and sure-handed second baseman Roberto Alomar, the Orioles won their division in both 1996 and 1997, reaching the ALCS both times. However, the Yankees bounced the Orioles in the 1996 ALCS, four games to one, and in 1997, the Cleveland Indians, sparked by slugging first baseman Jim Thome, stopped the Orioles four games to two.

The 1998 season marked the beginning of a new era for the Orioles—but not one the team wanted to enter. Baltimore started a decade-long slide in which even hitting the .500 mark would prove impossible. The organization had strayed from the Oriole Way and instead had gotten into the expensive habit of signing free agents—such as designated hitter Joe Carter in 1998 and outfielder Albert Belle in 1999—to shore up weak areas. Signing veterans in the late stages of their careers left the team with a huge payroll, few young impact players, and an uphill battle to get back to the top.

CENTER FIELDER · **BRADY ANDERSON**

Sometimes called the most unlikely 50-home-run hitter in baseball history, Brady Anderson turned heads in 1996, his eighth season in Baltimore. Never before or after did he top 24 home runs in a year, but during that 1996 season, his bat was on fire. The 32-year-old put up a .297 average with 50 home runs and 110 RBI, surpassing Frank Robinson as the Orioles' record holder for home runs in a season. Anderson was more than just a one-year power surge, however; his speed made him a fine defensive center fielder and helped him steal a club-record 307 bases in his career.

BRADY ANDERSON
CENTER FIELDER

BALTIMORE
ORIOLES

STATS

Orioles seasons: 1988–2001

Height: 6-foot-1

Weight: 185

- **3-time All-Star**

- **.989 career fielding percentage**

- **1,062 career runs scored**

- **3-time AL leader in times hit by pitch**

EARNING THEIR WINGS

In the midst of the team's slide, Ripken's achievements continued to be a bright spot. He reached 400 home runs in 1999 and 3,000 hits in 2000, making him 1 of only 7 major-leaguers ever to reach both milestones. At the beginning of the 2001 season, the superstar shortstop announced that his 21st season would be his last. "Cal's retirement brings an end to one of the finest, most noble careers this game has ever seen," said Orioles Hall-of-Famer Brooks Robinson.

Ripken's departure deepened the void of star power that had been created when Mussina jumped to the higher-paying Yankees in 2000. The Orioles continued to post losing records, finishing fourth in the tough AL East every year from 1998 to 2003. Right fielder Jay Gibbons impressed fans with his 28 home runs in 2002, but he clearly needed more support on the field for the team to succeed. And in 2004, he got it, as the Orioles acquired both hot-hitting catcher Javy Lopez and smooth shortstop Miguel Tejada, who had won the AL MVP award in 2002.

The additions paid dividends immediately. Lopez hit .316 in 2004,

CAL RIPKEN JR.

bashing 23 home runs and driving in 86 runs. Tejada, who seemed to hit best with players in scoring position, set a new team record with an AL-high 150 RBI. The Orioles rose to third place in the AL East, although their 78–84 record was still under the .500 mark. "This is a good, good ballclub," manager Lee Mazzilli said. "This is a club that can compete with any team in the league."

Hoping to add one more big stick to the lineup, the Orioles traded for disgruntled Chicago Cubs slugger Sammy Sosa in 2005. But Sosa's

THE HOME RUN THAT WASN'T

In the eighth inning of Game 1 of the 1996 ALCS, the Orioles were clinging to a one-run lead over the Yankees. Then New York's star shortstop, Derek Jeter, hit a high fly ball to deep right field. The crowd at Yankee Stadium rose to its feet, hoping that the ball would reach the stands—but Baltimore outfielder Tony Tarasco drifted back toward the wall, confident that he could make the catch. Just as Tarasco reached up to glove the ball for the out, a 12-year-old Yankees fan reached over the fence, got his hand on the ball, and made it bounce back into the stands. Right-field umpire Rich Garcia ruled it a

home run, despite protests by Tarasco and the Orioles. The Yankees went on to win that game in extra innings and to top the Orioles four games to one in the series. Garcia later conceded that the fan had interfered with the ball but asserted that Tarasco wouldn't have caught it anyway. The following year, the Yankees installed a railing to prevent future interference, but that action was too late to appease Baltimore manager Davey Johnson. "It was a real big game, and we were going to win it," Johnson said. "That changed a lot of things."

RIGHT FIELDER · PAUL BLAIR

An outstanding defensive outfielder, Paul Blair was known for his ability to get back on the deepest fly balls, a skill that allowed him to play a shallow outfield and take away many base hits. His best year at the plate was 1969, when he hit for a .285 average with 26 home runs and 76 RBI. But his consistency and speed put him in the top five in club history in doubles, triples, and stolen bases. Blair was a crucial part of the Orioles' World Series teams of the 1960s and '70s, making several spectacular catches in key playoff games.

PAUL BLAIR
RIGHT FIELDER

BALTIMORE
ORIOLES

STATS

Orioles seasons: 1964–76

Height: 6 feet

Weight: 171

- **2-time All-Star**

- **8-time Gold Glove winner**

- **171 career stolen bases**

- **282 career doubles**

MANAGER · EARL WEAVER

A colorful character with a vast knowledge of baseball, Earl Weaver won 1,480 games as a big-league manager, putting him 21st on the all-time wins list as of 2010. He managed 18 seasons—all for the Orioles. Weaver led the team to the World Series four times, coming away with a world championship in 1970. Never a fan of "small ball," Weaver liked to have powerful hitters in his lineup and pitchers who could hold the other team down. Weaver is perhaps most remembered for his fiery demeanor; he set a major-league record by being ejected from 98 games, including both ends of a doubleheader in 1985.

EARL WEAVER
MANAGER

BALTIMORE
ORIOLES

STATS

Orioles seasons as manager:
   1968–82, 1985–86

Managerial record: 1,480–1,060

World Series championship: 1970

Baseball Hall of Fame inductee
   (1996)

best years were behind him when he donned Baltimore orange and black. The once-feared slugger hit just .221 with 14 home runs before retiring after the season. Distracted by off-field controversies—including allegations of steroid use against longtime first baseman Palmeiro—and slowed by injuries to key players, the team ended 2005 back in fourth place.

A winning season seemed within reach in 2006 as new manager Sam Perlozzo relied on the formidable nucleus of Tejada, Lopez, and second baseman Brian Roberts. Baltimore played .500 ball during the first two months of the season but slid down the standings by the end of September and finished the year 70–92.

Pitcher Erik Bedard, who topped the AL with 221 strikeouts, and right fielder Nick Markakis, who led the team with 112 RBI, tried to keep the 2007 Orioles from becoming the third team in major-league history to post 10 straight losing seasons. But with Tejada

NICK MARKAKIS

Nick Markakis was a multidimensional standout, displaying a powerful swing at the plate, good speed on the bases, and sound defense in the field.

BRIAN MATUSZ

sidelined with a broken wrist bone, Baltimore stumbled down the stretch, winning only 11 of its final 39 games and posting a disappointing 69–93 record.

In an effort to rebuild once again, the team traded away Tejada and Bedard before the start of the 2008 season. Jeremy Guthrie stepped up to take over Bedard's position as the club's pitching ace, tallying 10 wins to lead the team in both 2008 and 2009. Unfortunately, his league-leading 17 losses in 2009 garnered more attention, and the Orioles tumbled to last place in 2008, 2009, and 2010. But Guthrie, young pitcher Brian Matusz, and hard-hitting outfielders Adam Jones and Luke Scott planned to escape the AL East cellar soon. "[Baltimore] has been kind

ORIOLES

A FAMILY AFFAIR

When one thinks about famous baseball families, certain names spring to mind. There were great father-son combos such as Bobby and Barry Bonds and Ken Griffey Sr. and Jr. One family, the Boones, even managed to put three generations in the big leagues. But the Baltimore Orioles franchise can pride itself on being the only team ever to feature two brothers who were managed by their father at the major-league level. From 1988 to 1992, the Orioles' double-play combo consisted of Cal Ripken Jr. at shortstop and his younger brother Bill at second base. (The brothers were on the official roster together for the first time in 1987, although they did not become the starting middle infield duo until the next season.) Cal Ripken Sr. managed the team for the entirety of the 1987 season but was fired only six games into the 1988 campaign. He had spent 36 years in the Baltimore organization as a minor-league player, scout, coach, and manager. Cal Jr. enjoyed a 21-year career with the club, and Bill spent a total of 7 seasons wearing an Orioles uniform. Perhaps no family has contributed as much to a major-league franchise as the Ripkens have to the Orioles.

CAL JR.

CAL SR.

BILL

Big outfielders Adam Jones (left) and Luke Scott (opposite) combined to slug nearly 50 home runs in 2010 to boost an improving Orioles offense.

ADAM JONES

of the hidden city over the last decade," said Jones, who won a Gold Glove award in 2009. "We have a very good team. It's young and raw, but I think we have a very good team."

Baltimore has had many good teams over the course of its long history, including seven that made it all the way to the World Series and three that hoisted baseball's greatest prize. Even in the club's down seasons, fans have found heroes in whom they could put their hope and feats in which they could take pride. As today's Orioles take flight in beautiful Camden Yards, both players and fans remain hopeful that orange and black will soon be the colors of champions once more.

LUKE SCOTT

INDEX

AL pennants 9, 19, 26
All-Star Game 31
Alomar, Roberto 34
Altobelli, Joe 26
Anderson, Brady 29, 34, 35
Baldschun, Jack 20
Baseball Hall of Fame 8, 14, 20, 27, 28, 40
Bauer, Hank 19
Bedard, Erik 41, 44
Belanger, Mark 18, 21
Belle, Albert 34
Blair, Paul 21, 39
Bumbry, Al 25
Carter, Joe 34
Cuellar, Mike 21, 22, 24, 25
Cy Young Award 8, 24
DeCinces, Doug 25
Dempsey, Rick 29
division championships 21, 22, 25, 26, 34
Dobson, Pat 22, 24, 25
Estrada, Chuck 16
Flanagan, Mike 25, 29
Gaedel, Eddie 12
Gibbons, Jay 36
Gold Glove award 14, 16, 18, 21, 27, 28, 39, 47
Guthrie, Jeremy 44
Hansen, Ron 16
Hoiles, Chris 13
Johnson, Davey 18, 21, 38
Jones, Adam 44, 47
Lopez, Javy 36–37, 41
Lowenstein, John 25, 30
major-league records 14, 28, 29, 34, 40
Markakis, Nick 41
Martinez, Dennis 25, 29
Matusz, Brian 44
Mazzilli, Lee 37
McGregor, Scott 29
McNally, Dave 19, 22, 24, 25
Memorial Stadium 10, 33
Miranda, Willie 10
Murray, Eddie 14, 25, 29
Mussina, Mike 29, 36

MVP award 16, 20, 27, 28, 36
Oriole Park at Camden Yards 31, 33, 47
"Oriole Way" 15, 34
Palmeiro, Rafael 33, 34, 41
Palmer, Jim 8, 19, 21, 22, 24, 25, 29
Pappas, Milt 16, 20
Perlozzo, Sam 41
playoffs 14, 18, 21, 22, 25, 26, 30, 34, 38
    AL Championship Series 21, 22, 26, 30, 34, 38
Powell, Boog 21, 25
retired numbers 27
Richards, Paul 15
Ripken, Bill 45
Ripken, Cal Jr. 26, 27, 28, 29, 33–34, 36, 45
Ripken, Cal Sr. 26, 45
Roberts, Brian 41
Robinson, Brooks 15–16, 19, 21, 22, 25, 27, 36
Robinson, Frank 16, 19, 20, 21, 25, 29, 35
    Triple Crown 16, 19, 20
Rookie of the Year award 14, 26, 28
St. Louis Browns 6, 9–10, 12
    relocation to Baltimore 10
Scott, Luke 44
Simpson, Dick 20
Singleton, Ken 25
Sosa, Sammy 37, 41
Sportsman's Park 10
Stephens, Vern 9, 10
Tarasco, Tony 38
Taylor, Zack 12
team name 10
team records 8, 21, 35, 37
Tejada, Miguel 36, 37, 41, 44
Triandos, Gus 10
Veeck, Bill 9–10, 12
Weaver, Earl 19, 21, 22, 26, 40
Wilhelm, Hoyt 16
Williams, Ken 9
Woodling, Gene 10
world championships 19, 20, 22, 29, 30, 40, 47
World Series 8, 9, 19, 20, 22, 24, 25, 26, 27, 29, 30, 39, 40, 47

ORIOLES